Little Knives

Little Knives

Poems by

Dara-Lyn Shrager

Cover design by Shay Culligan
Cover image by Tema Stauffer
Author photo by Laura Pedrick Photography

ISBN: 979-8-90146-707-7
Library of Congress Control Number: 2026932859

Kelsay Books
502 South 1040 East, A-119
American Fork, Utah 84003
Kelsaybooks.com

More Praise for Little Knives

There's nothing little about these knives, these seasoned scalpels cutting minutia to discover what's most tender and delicate. What I admire most about this book is in the way it honors familial legacies both worthy and ajar. *Little Knives* is a reminder to study. To squint in the dark and discover the demon who traipses like a lithe ballerina, one step, two step, three step—leap.

—Luke Johnson, author of *Distributary*

In these vibrant poems of biography, Shrager showcases a true talent for imbuing the smallest human details with authenticity and layered meanings. Each poem maps out the human heart in relation to that larger earth heart, in all their internal conflicts, with precision and grace. Overflowing with vivid language, *Little Knives* is both intellectually stimulating and emotionally engaging, reminding us of the beautiful complexities of being human.

—John Sibley Williams, author of *The Drowning House*

Acknowledgments

Dear reader, don't feel guilty for skipping this part if you don't yet know me, but I cannot complete this book without expressing gratitude to certain people for the love, patience and support they generously offered to me during the years these poems took to find the page.

Thank you to Danny, Max, Scott, Sondra and Norman because you are the poems. Thank you to Rachel because you are my closest confidant and the best editor I know.

Thank you to Rachel Marie Patterson, Nicole Callihan, Charlotte Pence, Luke Johnson and John Sibley Williams for being such excellent poets that I wanted blurbs from you. Thank you to my tennis friends for listening to me babble in fragments during Tuesday morning drill. I like to work out poem-things while improving my backhand, and the Pretty Brook players have tolerated years of this. Thank you to my revered yoga instructors for leading me back to my center when I have drifted away. And last but of utmost importance, thank you dear reader. My poems make me, remake me, unmake me and make me again. It all feels very intimate and important. I so appreciate your presence here among my most precious things.

Thank you to the following publications, in which versions of these poems previously appeared, sometimes with different titles:

Another Chicago Magazine: "Christmastime at the Mall," "Drift," "High Tide," "September," "Waffle"
Atticus Review: "Rupture"
Banyan Review: "King Georges Road," "Seeds," "Rough," "Next Door to Fantasia Grooming Salon"

Barnstorm Journal: "Beth Israel"
Braving the Body Anthology: "Wednesday Bronchitis"
Breakwater Review: "One-Eared Greyhound"
The Broadkill Review: "Ply Mar Swim Club"
Crab Creek Review: "Morphs of the Eastern Screech Owl"
Hayden's Ferry Review: "Silver Hill"
Heavy Feather Review: "California"
The Iowa Review: "Camp Wohelo, 1979"
The Los Angeles Review: "Grounded"
MER: "Twenty-One"
Moon City Review: "Lockdown"
Pacifica Literary Review: "Little Knives"
Painted Bride Quarterly: "Belladonna"
Pembroke Magazine: "Illusion"
River Heron Review: "Shoes"
The Rupture: "Silver Lake"
Solstice Literary Magazine: "Narrow Valley"
South Dakota Review: "The Perfect Summer"
Split Rock Review: "Knotted Wrack"
SWWIM Every Day: "Sunday Ritual"
West Trade Review: "Stillbirth"
West Trestle Review: "Faint"

Contents

III. MILK CARTON HEART

I.
THE BARBED FENCE LINE

Swallowtail

My father stored metal fasteners
in baby food jars. I roamed our
little town, collecting silver washers
and rusty nails. Every lane named
for a member of King Arthur's Court.
His praise I chose to hear as love.
In his workroom, a vice bolted to a table,
red paint worn away where his hands
turned a thick pin to close the jaws.
I crushed things when he wasn't home:
quarter, fork, tiger swallowtail,
my right index finger. In middle age,
I dream my father as a boy, asleep
by the sea, floating from sand to sky.
I cannot sit down with the first man
who hurt me. Being woundable,
I am a butterfly pressed into a vice.

Faint

My mother's purse strap catches
a door handle, slams her facedown
on cold concrete. All these years
watching her progress from house
to car in case of days like these.
Now her coat sleeves make life
dangerous. It's not this season
that takes her so far from feeling,
but all the bitter ones. Into the phone,
I repeat words twice, three times,
until she grunts. She understands
or just wants me to stop. How
her eyes water. Her lips are dry.
Her ribs shake. I want to swaddle her
the way she swaddled me in the sunny
kitchen, Cream of Rice bubbling
over low flame. She cooked with milk
instead of water because she wanted
me to taste what's sweet. Nobody
can get half the warmth they need.

Terhune Orchards

County Highway 1, duck blind,
I catch a warning with my eye—
Caution: High Pressure Pipeline.
Dread, as when a sparrow flies
directly at the windowpane.
I once asked my mother why
and she told little Dara, *fate.*

Call mom into the car's blank screen,
the weight of words a heavy thing.
I hunt for those she doesn't say:
precious girl, I miss, my love—
I am still small enough to hold
the rocking chair, a garland gold.
Ask time to wing me back to her.

Dormant Stayman Winesaps
shoot their branches crooked-high,
flame-red against a clement sky.
Time won't stop for me—not now—
a startled baby in my brain.
Someday soon, this pipe will burst
and set the apple trees aflame.

Next Door to Fantasia Grooming Salon

The postmaster lowers an American flag at precisely 4pm. It's a small display of pageantry; he never misses a day. His ceremony makes me wonder if Brownies still assemble in sashes with badges and brown skorts to pay their dues: *clink-clink, clank-clank, golden money in the bank.* A circle of good deeds earns a pin. The groomer slips a loop over my dog's head with her three-fingered hand. Something about lupus and drugs pushed through a port in her neck. My old dog's eyes are milky with age and though her teeth have long since rotted away, she nips. I leave them to their routine and look through a window caked with fur, at a fat squirrel running the length of a power line. What in this tired corner of town is not a small machine.

One-Eared Greyhound

Translucent that delicate flesh,
blue-collared brindle on stilts,
spirals of breath doubling out
his snout into this wintry mix
of fever and fear. Pink flap
where a second ear should be.
Half of every sound dead
to him, squirrel-scratch and fish-flip
and somebody far away
calling his name. Half the news
we mute, the other half we cannot
stop repeating. How we long
to be warm, taken somewhere
by loving hands and stroked to sleep.

Morphs of the Eastern Screech Owl

for Jeremy

A bird is hatched a certain morph
and remains that color all its life.
Red morph owls do not survive as often
as the grey. I was reckless enough to assume
that a college student who goes to sleep
in his single bed will rise again to dress
his body and see the day. Spinnaker-
winged, man-faced bird: yesterday,
I saw you startle from an evergreen.
Your eyes liquid gold. Now, your body
is a brown paper bag, crushed to the curb.
Bits of you lift and blow in circles across
the double yellow line. What a thing to bury
a boy. To stand around his coffin eating
Sanchez hoagies from his best-loved shop.
To look down at dusk and see the shadow
of someone miraculous cross overhead.

King Georges Road

Consider the red fox.
A week ago, he slipped
into a meadow of ryegrass
and Kentucky blue. Now
his body slung over the curb
shows no signs of injury
but is ruptured, spleen-bled.
Winter coat of auburn,
paws ink-dipped. Creature
with a belly so white and clean.
What god made more
than one of any thing
so pristine? Left his body
for the carrion crows.

Marblehead

After a winter entombed,
I emerge into a spring
of busted bird nests, newspaper
bricks amid leggy vines
of mint. Rain carves arteries
into the softening fescue
and a certain stench reveals
raccoon bones licked clean.
In this New England, where
women deemed too nervous
for the home once got locked
away and given clay. Here, I find
pebbled shards of green, ochre,
blue. In a bucket I gather them,
rinse until mud clots melt away.
I glue them back together.
Quarter and half vessels
which hold no water, stems,
half-open buds, only faded
colors where they once shined
with promise from the kiln.

Narrow Valley

I arrive at the frozen glen
in a violet hour. New Englanders
keep to themselves, especially
in winter. Each house contains
its calamities like canned peaches
in the cellar. The first piece
cut from my niece's flank,
the second from a hiding space
behind her ribs. When a body
opens, heat rises and fogs
the glasses of anyone peering
inside. Was it a fox that shredded
the hen? A red bandit picks
along the perimeter of the barn.
A nick is all it takes
to drain a child's vena cava.
In a far field, cutting horses paw
at the green. A mare nickers
to her foal wobbling
at the barbed fence line.

Little Knives

That bruised fist clenches
again in my niece's chest.
A surgeon fishes a guide wire
through her thigh, lighting
a path to her stuttering heart.

All the little knives will come,
cut her before she's done.

One year ago, doctors slapped
a map of her body on a screen.
Treasure hunt for cancer.
X marks the spots where
a scalpel will slice away
part of everything she needs,
or doesn't, as the case
may be. A miracle, I think,
her body a canvas of stars.

She will live, I say. Why not
this brown-haired girl
with the neck of a swan
and the nearly soundless way
she enters a room?

Scale

Yes, I’m a fish, catch of the day,
presented on a white plate.
A diamond ray with one
marbled eye turned skyward
and one steam-sealed to a dish.
An otherwise quite common fish,
christened, then whisked back
into the clattered kitchen.

Maybe I will not grow old.
It’s possible my puckered bag
of scales can resist the knife’s
edge. If not, lift the backbone
from my body. Balance
the constellation of my vertebrae
in your hands. Trace my lips
with one finger, torn sideways
by the barb.

High Tide

I wade into the bruised and swollen
sea where rugs of ribbon kelp
entwine my ankles. The current
drags me in and holds me under.
In the salt wash, flashes of diamond
light spin into my final scene.
I descend, finally free, in the murky
deep, tumbling through pinwheels
of sand, fumbling for the golden band
that has slipped so icy from my finger.
Eel grass, brittle stars, white flecks
of bone scour me in this green abyss.

Drift

The old trawler rests at anchor
east of Forchue Island. My eyes
are fixed on the horizon as I slip
into the sea. Sergeant majors,
yellowtail, a solitary glassy sweeper—
they all drift the radiant surface.
Deeper down, spotted spiny lobsters
slumber, curled in beds of jagged rocks,
their eye stalks swaying in the wake
my flippers make. Tube sponges
exhale waste through gaping mouths.
Fukushima, Three-Mile Island, Newark.
My mind is a net with one doomed
notion, shrinking, and then invisible.
Everywhere, this dying hooks me.

Knotted Wrack

This morning, millions of ghost crabs
spray the beach, arranged by some sequence
of moons. Their opaque claws, each smaller
than a droplet, serrated with godly precision.
Knobbed whelk, shark eye, slippersnail,
all tangled in knotted wrack.
Creatures populate a swath of sand
or run desperate alongside a cargo plane.
Bodies in the fuel-wake of a C-17
so massive, it carries hundreds away
but leaves thousands behind. Today,
Bagram Airbase became a morgue.
Nature makes the mollusk and the man.
The pilot who drowns out cries
with the engine's roar. Low tide sweeps
a million blinking blue mussels back
into the green mouth of the sea. From the sky,
bright dots of color might be mistaken
for flowers, sprouting through cracks
in the runway. Or human bodies,
flailing their arms at the roiling sky.

II.
BRING BACK THE NOISE AND STINK OF BOYS

Stillbirth

Early in the season, I say
daughter is gone. I don't say
dead, just gone. Terrycloth
swaddles hang next to my coat.
Inside this house where
everything shifts on bad hips.
Sleeping dog paddles through dreams.
Tongues click in heating vents—
try to sleep through such a sound.
Scribble of branches against glass.
No preschool hieroglyphics
etched on the nursery wall.
Wolf Moon pouring its yolk
into an empty crib.

Rupture

When I leaned over the side of my bed,
they were standing in a field of poppies,
nurses in blue scrubs, doctors in green.
Their hands were wedged under my body
hemorrhaging. Something blue and plastic
jabbed my arm, the baby blanketed away.
Sign here, said a doctor, handing
my husband a pen. Then wheeled me
through a cold, white forest of clear vines.
A voice near my head insisted I open
my eyes, bear witness to this little death.
In recovery, a morning show blared,
celebrity chef deboning a chicken.
Stabbed through, I demanded my newborn
back to me. *Open your eyes.* When I did,
I saw nurses skating by on slippered feet.
My body shrouded by new white sheets,
fixed to silver machines.

Beth Israel

The baby arrived with legs
that swung out like doors set
backwards on their hinges.
Across from the building where
he was born, another building
to tell us *he will walk*
or *no.* So we went, wrapped
in scarves against the sideways
snow. Just one day after that
blue coil sprung away from him
then back, dropping onto my belly
with a wet thud. And the red
river pooling in the shallows
where the floor was worn,
painting the soles of white clogs
dancing all around my hospital
bed. I did not feel the pouring
but I imagined I could. That next
day, faces stamped blank. We rode
the escalator that swallowed
its own silver teeth. If you have ever
stolen anything then you know how
we left that place, hunched over
our new possession, eyes down,
mouths tight, ready to sprint
if anyone called our names.

Belladonna

I tighten a Biliblanket
around my newborn
then nurse him. Too-short
electrical cord—
I lie on the rug to let him
catch. A small anger flowers
in me as I run two fingers down
the nubs of his spine, counting
as I go. Guzzle, gasp, swallow.
Sticky, yellow beads dot
the receiving blanket beneath
his jaundiced limbs.
My body pulls away,
wishes to rise to the quilt
and downy pillows on my bed.
We are only halfway through.
Glow worm grows weary
of latching, hollers at my breast
and the Velcro belt squeezing
light into his skin. After,
he naps under weak sun
splitting in through window
blinds. *Plink, plink* in the yard
below. Shiny black berries
drop their death
from bell-shaped blooms.

Christmastime at the Mall

Inside the overheated atrium,
a giant sleigh overflows
with synthetic snow. Forever
white and, when touched,
dissolves into a million
toxic particles. I hear a wasp
rattling inside my baby's ribs.
How it hums his death song.

In the meantime, he kicks
at withered balloons, grinds
Cheerios into his stroller seat,
wheezes his eyes bloodshot.

So it's back to the nebulizer
and the crib, sticky with yesterday's
milk. His hands form into fists
while he sleeps. Back at the mall,
the sleigh's golden runners sway
each time the heat growls awake.

Waffle

Always one puffed waffle
on the highchair tray. My baby
picks with his pinchers, pops
pieces onto his outstretched
tongue. Little reptile, parked
near the oven where it's warm,
where I sip soda to kill the hours.
Traces of frozen blueberry
on his face, my own fingertips
stained. The forecast will hold nothing
but space before an ice storm
slices my grown boy sideways.
He will know the moment
he loses control, water pouring
through the window seals.
He will swim into the frozen dark.
Four-hundred miles away, I will freeze,
forget the pot boiling over. Nothing
will happen to save his life.

The Kitchen

for Martha Rhodes

In the green highchair, a baby screams,
bare-chested beneath a Velcro harness,
positioned to face the sink. Behind
him, a screen door flaps open. May
birds skittle and sing. When a car door
creaks, the baby grips the plastic tray
on which noodles swim in butter
and drool, twists his diapered middle
and his neck—where apple juice
runs in rivulets—to see if he can see
his mother coming in. Or to catch her
leaving. Another tiny death. Moments
ago, he was stuffing his own fat hand
into his mouth with gnawing hunger.
Now he howls and strains, this little
prisoner of appetites. What he loves
most, out of view.

Lockdown

The double doors are chain-locked
and greasy with fingerprints.
Inside the red brick building,
the principal answers a beige desk
phone. I have called the emergency
number to say, *I'm here,* panicking
near bicycles racked in midday sun.
A man has breached the middle
school, claims he has a gun.
Send out my second-born son.
In the hour before his birth, a nurse
made toast for me. I ate two triangles
with strawberry jam. Then I bled
the boy and my own body within
death's soundless reach. No more
time to whittle every hope I have.
Is that his honeyed hair I see,
beneath a half-moon desk
soldered to a metal chair?

Illusion

We enter a monarchy by way of Øresund
Bridge. The city of Malmö recedes, its ear
curled to the Sound. Tracks drop into tunnel
and we're pulled under the sea. In this vacuum,
my boy laughs in a dream. False night illuminates
the fingerprints he left on an oval window.

A boy in a railcar doesn't lean on his mother
forever. By twelve, he'll sharpen into locks
and passcodes. For now, he is close. I count
the hook scars above the arch of his brow.
Luck flips in my stomach like a netted fish.
He'll wake into a country of black gulls.

September

The first dead leaves of summer
curl into fists on the blacktop.
I cannot leave this open window
through which I watch my son
packing the pickup truck—
six plastic storage bins,
an unassembled bookcase,
a Lavoie ski poster from Montreal.
How I yearn to hear the hum
of his animal body just a while longer.
Second born, who rose without
regard for my body recoiling.
What do I hold now if not that
baby boy? A plastic bag of hangers
he waves off, steering the truck
across the lawn, racing to get
some place where I'm not
slicing potatoes for stew.

Rough

In which mess hall do you eat three squares,
my son? At home, it has been so quiet, save
a parade of red-bellied woodpeckers, as upright
as soldiers at attention.

Let fly the colors!

They rocket upward before landing
to split seeds from hulls. After we agreed
that silence was our only way forward,
you called a truce, traveled home for hugs.
I must have smiled because my teeth
brushed the shoulder of your fatigues,
leaving me cotton-mouthed.

About face.

You call me rough where I see myself
smooth. The first nest of the season failed
because I ruined it with a curious broom.
What I have learned is birds mark time.

Rest on arms reversed.

Seeds

It was supposed to be the season
for carving pumpkins and nesting
in against the cold, but weeks
of warm weather spoiled the big
orange gourd. The smaller one,
a milky white gibbous moon,
refused to rot. In its hollow,
a kingdom of spider mites gorged
on pulp. By mid-November,
the empty eyes filled with mold.
And its toothy smile turned frown
went slack-jawed gape. I half-
believed that pumpkin would last
the winter. That my boy could return
to a place where little changed.
But time can be understood
by watching chunks of pith collapse
into browning grass. The salted seeds
shivered when we toasted them.

California

The weeping cherry trees behind our house
were once no taller than kindergarten boys
colliding plastic trucks on a carpet of EZ grass.
Now, giant leaf canopies block the sun.
There's just the lone dog out there, chasing
sudden whips of wind. Deep beneath my collar,
I feel cold. Hungry for those half-eaten
bowls of Cheerios left bloating by the kitchen
sink. Bring back the filthy sneakers, piled high
by the dented mud room door. Bring back
the noise and stink of boys, their long seasons
of runny noses and handprints on the walls.
With a dry mouth, I answer some late version
of a phone. I have been searching for my boy.
He was driving out in an arid canyon, where
snakes seek the shade of boulders, glisten
bright when they shed their skins to grow.

National Gypsum Day

It’s time to ride our bikes down the silver
sidewalks of our town. Why don’t you
walk the dog with bright blue baggies
knotted along the leash like flags
while wet plaster falls in clots off new
steel beams? Just look at these squares
in the not-yet-walls where windows might
someday hang. Holidays are hard. No one
likes a handmade sign reading *Closed Today*.
But listen: we cannot put the earth back
as we found it, so let’s keep digging!
Let’s spend another hazy three-day weekend
gluing sheets of spangled crystals
to wooden frames. Let’s make everything
red, white, and blue.

Silver Lake

I have brought my suitcases to the West Coast,
where people drink lattes in the sunshine
and small dogs pee on 2x2 pads of Astroturf.
Fresh air falls into the reservoir, except when
smoke chokes the San Gabriel mountains.
Some days, I have to stop speaking just
to save my breath. I've followed my son
to California because, back home,
I am shrinking. Here, among lemon trees
and dry brush, neighbors share shady
courtyards and stackable washer/dryers,
tucked outdoors under fitted sheets. One last try
to be a woman who sheds her flannel sadness.
After midnight, I walk the terrier along Sunset,
pull him past taco wrappers flattened to the street.
Neon lights bathe each face in manufactured beauty.

Silver Hill

in the waiting room   metal chairs devour
their own legs   tables chained together
each row of chairs and tables a row
from which a body cannot free itself
my son   briefly there   then not   I am
making animal sounds   and a list
#7   a lock snapping shut
#8   my neck a narrow pane
somewhere I hear my son
then not
walkie-talkies beeping pagers khakis
buzzing silver phones   a white coat
slides a dixie cup of drinking water
down my bolted row   time to finish
the list   #9   I will not let them
#10   if they do I will not let my eyes

Twenty-One

My firstborn cradled every red-eyed
cicada in a Dixie cup, their soft bodies
electric jewels, settled in a field hospital
of tiny cots, fashioned from cosmetic
squares. A waxed and cushioned world.

Seventeen years later, he rarely calls
home but my name is still mother.
When he falters, I drive to his apartment
in the metal north, into the clang
of a city with its trapdoors and sooted
drifts. A week's worth of mail blocks
the door. The tenderness in each of us
cannot survive without a tiny bit of care.
I water the pincushion cactus where
its pink eyes have withered shut.

I miss the white stove, warm tub,
buttered noodles. I tell my son that twenty-one
should feel something like powerful.
He answers, *trying*.

Sunday Ritual

We FaceTime just before sunset.
After, you'll thread the hills, look
down over the basin and catch what
you will of yips and howls. With
the hazards, maybe you won't crash
the Jeep. It's something we share,
a thoroughly modern way to be mother
and son. The dead hour at In-N-Out
Burger, then home to your half of a rented
bed. You can't remember how I climbed
into the star-strung crib and napped
a little with you, on a late afternoon
just like this, in the weak winter light,
together. You craning toward some
invisible edge and me, still bleeding
blades three months after your birth.
Hush, now, never.

Grounded

My son's newborn pirate robe
hangs dusty in the closet near
my winter coat. Shoulders silver
in the sunlight when I pull the hanger
to breathe him. In dreams, I long
to fly over the city in which he lands
to play a concert then lift off again.
Just type any letter of the alphabet
so I'll know you're ok. He sends
a *g* or a *j*. It's not the clock's fault
I am more dented metal than lucent
wings. Twenty years ago, I scrubbed
sweet potato stains from onesies,
deaf to the second hand setting
my pulse to his own. No way
to know this engine would slowly
power down. A palm to the white
wood of his childhood bedroom
door. I am beginning again without
love. Each turn spins my body
toward what hollow, I cannot say.

Shoes

Two pairs of snowshoes and a hand-drawn map
to Hitch Creek Road. Now the mountain's
grand right shoulder, just ahead. See the soft,
bright bands of muscle braided there, the wide,
frozen valleys we traverse. Where quaking aspens
shine their leaves and fresh powder clings
to each green song. A man could snowshoe
two steps to either side and disappear through
white door after white door after white door.
Or slip from binding straps and step right
down through a floor in the snow. Down to
the sudden eternal eventide. Where clouds
curl into plumes of sugared light. In a sky more
than twice the size of any other. Yes, it's possible
to pretend we aren't falling.

III.
MILK CARTON HEART

Camp Wohelo, 1979

After Barry Manilow's "Even Now"

My Panasonic Take 'N' Tape
needed 4 C batteries to spin
its furry wheels around. After just
one week, those batteries died.
Even though I packed two Barry
Manilow cassettes and John Denver's
Greatest Hits, all summer long,
I listened to just one song.
My counselor didn't wear underpants
and her name was Jane. To punish
my homesickness: no batteries,
no canteen. I held my shiny Panasonic
like a fat baby and licked a river
of snot. Every night after Lights Out,
I tucked the music to my ear, pressed
my body against cinder blocks,
ran my finger through rough canals
and bled. I conjured my mother
patting her face with Laszlo of Paris
perfumed powder. Two weeks in,
I surrendered to sleep. When I woke
to the bugle, my bunkmates roared
and pointed to the maxi pads stuck
to my cot's metal frame.

The Litter

My mother with her fists full
of weeds and three kittens to bury
out back. Grey milk leaked
from their bodies into the vine-bound
earth. She plunged a metal shovel
so deep, it left a tang on my tongue.
Now my sons are leaving home.
How to stop the ruin, how not
to sit swollen and stung. How did
my mother resist the hush
behind our house, its promise
to seal her in sleep? No wonder
she courts the surgeon's knife.
We want the permanent wound.

The Perfect Summer

After Hurricane Agnes, moss grew
on railroad ties. Inside every truck
tire swing, tiny rafts of mosquito
eggs drifted in rainwater.

All that slippery-slimy June,
Mother drove figure eights
through the parking lot
at Plymouth Elementary.

Oh, how I loved to roller skate,
holding onto a back fin
of the family's two-tone Oldsmobile.

The spell broke when my brother
screamed, *Get up, get up!*
That Oldsmobile saddled the length
of me. I heard *trying* in my throat,
thought *heavy* is just a word.

And my brother, who never said hi
at school, suddenly whispered
in my ear, *please don't move.*

A frightened finch is just a bird,
but also a mother, flapping wildly
at the wheel. Much later, my body
atop a quilt of poppy blooms.
My head grew a red balloon.

I watched the Olympics on TV.
People from Israel got taken
hostage, then shot. Stiff towels
sopped my blood. Mother
swallowed tiny pink pills
with warm ginger ale
the man with blue bottles
placed next to my bed.
Summer slid away
in a morphine haze.

Jack-in-the-Box

Mother stirred catsup into ground beef
popping in a frying pan, told me
about brain cancer. Grease bubbles shot
against the backsplash. After dinner,
I went to my room, turned the little red
handle. *All around the mulberry bush,*
the monkey chased the weasel.
After school the next day, I ran all the way
to the Sloanes' wood-paneled den—
a cave until I opened the door
and sunlight screamed into the room.
Mrs. Sloane was lying in a bed
I'd never seen before, her body gowned
beneath green blankets, her head
a papier-mâché. And Mr. Sloane—
his face redder than a burn—
rushed toward the white light piercing.
So much for pulling the Jack-in-the-Box
from my knapsack and making everyone
laugh. No place for a jester stuffed inside
a tin box. Or a girl with her mouth agape.

Wednesday Bronchitis

With a throat full of swords and a milk-carton heart,
she walks a mile to the mall, crosses at the four-way

light on Plymouth Turnpike, putting her whole hand
inside the broken metal mouth of a signal button

that once held the burn of summer and the bite
of frost in its wide "O." *Push,* she says to nobody,

then pilots her body, rotten with sick, over double
yellow lines. Four dollars will buy something nice.

The Plymouth Meeting Mall, 1976

Nothing better than that newly-built,
overheated cement village on dead
winter weekend days. Where I rubbed
away paint on the noses of carousel
horses. Latch-key kid, sneaking
through X-rated aisles at Spencer's
Gifts. I snickered as I laid out
moist dollar bills for the dead-eyed
cashier at Wee Three Records.
In Bamberger's, my hand-me-down
boot prints melted by glass bureaus
belted in chrome. Peppermint
Meltaways perspired under fluorescent
lights. Such grown-up luxuries.
So, I threw pennies into arcs of neon
green chlorine, atomized from a brass
crown of jets. Among parents holding
hands with their children and teenage
couples kissing their wishes, I stood
alone. In that moist and modern
climate, my eyes sparked and stung.

Field Trip

At the 7-Up Bottling Plant, I imagined
I could be another girl. Buzzing
with the promise of bubbles pushing
the lids off giant vats of pop, I pressed
the front of my body against the back
of my bus buddy's jacket. When my brother
took the third-grade field trip, he came home
with stories of drinking as much birch beer
as his belly could hold. But after everything—
the metallic screech of conveyor belts,
too-bright smiles of lipsticked women
jotting on clipboards—my neon soda fantasy
dissolved into sugar-hot vomit on the bus
ride back to Plymouth Elementary.

Balloons

for Amelia Granese

For 6th-grade graduation, Amelia wore
a white dress from the Toddler
Department at Hess. Our principal read
from a stack of 3 x 5 cards and Amelia
coughed herself purple straight through.

After Assembly, we lined up in the gym.
Scrape of metal legs on waxed wood,
Polaroid camera clicks and carnations
for every girl. I wanted to hug Amelia
but she was choking and waving at me.

Outside, we each got a red balloon,
slip of paper and a pen. *Write your wish
and, on three, let go!* Into an afternoon
more perfect than a postcard. Amelia
with her face turned upwards,

made brighter by impermanence.

The Fire

Seven sirens and an acrid stink,
but I ate the scrambled eggs Mother
made, hid clumps in my napkin.

After breakfast, my brother and I
stood on the driveway in our pajamas,
spit soot at petunias and feather rocks.

He wanted to sneak over to see
the Hall house burn. But Mother said
to sort our toys in case the Hall boys

wanted to play. Board games, records
(including all my 45s), Toy Wonder
typewriter, tiny toilet with real flushing

sound. I tried to ask what happens when
you wake up in a room of flames, but
Mother stamped her slippered foot *no.*

Kick the Can

Our fourth-grade gang
hid in trees, sheds, behind
old barns, under tarps of rotting
leaves. Tract-housing truants,
our eyes feral in the dark.

Once, I tried the backseat
of a Cadillac Coupe de Ville.

When we played, we wore
no shoes and stayed out very
late. Nancy Lee cried at every
little thing: a bottle smashed
against the curb, a smear of blood
across her knee. Me, I kept
things to myself—the man
who climbed into the driver's
seat turned around
and spit at me.

Hypotenuse

In his oily rec room, Mr. P. drew
angles on wide-ruled paper.
When he leaned forward to erase
my mistakes, our knees touched
under the white card table.
Stale coffee on his breath.
I hated myself for not tipping
the table and running away.
I could hear my mother clinking
a fork upstairs, where she ate cake
with Mrs. P. In order to pass
geometry, I needed all the points
and planes that Mr. P. could teach.
He cared about math, but also me.
Which boy might try to kiss me
in the dark. I ended the year with a "D."

Ply Mar Swim Club

I swam because my mother
liked to watch me win. I was a tomboy,
broad-shouldered and bulldog-low
to the ground. Before each meet,
I knelt to splash my flat chest and threw
two quick swipes over my bathing cap.

My mother laid on a blanket
uphill. She waved me over to sit
only when my brother drifted
away. I didn't know the ground beneath
her was nothing but fists of weeds.

By the starting block, I stretched
at the redwood picnic tables and licked
lime Jell-O powder from my palm.
My hair inking halos on the cement
between pool and snack bar.

I wanted my mother to notice me.
Like the time I held a French-fry high
and a horsefly landed on my finger.
A blood-blister rose where the bug's
mandibles pierced my skin.

To hide my tears, I laid on the hot
concrete, first on my belly then back.
Because my mother wanted
a beautiful girl, I wore my flowered
bathing suit, on which the elastic
had failed. A towel to hide my thighs.
I couldn't make anything fit.

About the Author

Dara-Lyn Shrager lives in Princeton, New Jersey and is the co-founder and editor of *Radar Poetry*. Her chapbook *The Boy from Egypt* was published in 2009 by Finishing Line Press. Her debut full-length collection *Whiskey, X-Ray, Yankee* was published by Barrow Street Press in 2018, after being named a finalist for the Barrow Street Poetry Prize.

Dara-Lyn holds an MFA from Bennington College and a BA from Smith College. Her poems appear or are forthcoming in many journals, including *The Iowa Review, The Los Angeles Review, Crab Creek Review, Hayden's Ferry Review, The Greensboro Review, Nashville Review, Passages North, Salamander* and *Yemassee.* Her poetry has been nominated for the Pushcart Prize and *Best of the Net* and also appears in the anthology *Braving the Body* (Harbor Editions, 2024).

Her articles have been published in newspapers and magazines including *The New York Times, The Philadelphia Inquirer* and *Philadelphia Magazine.*

www.ingramcontent.com/pod-product-compliance
Lightning Source LLC
LaVergne TN
LVHW090618110826
845146LV00001B/434

* 9 7 9 8 9 0 1 4 6 7 0 7 7 *